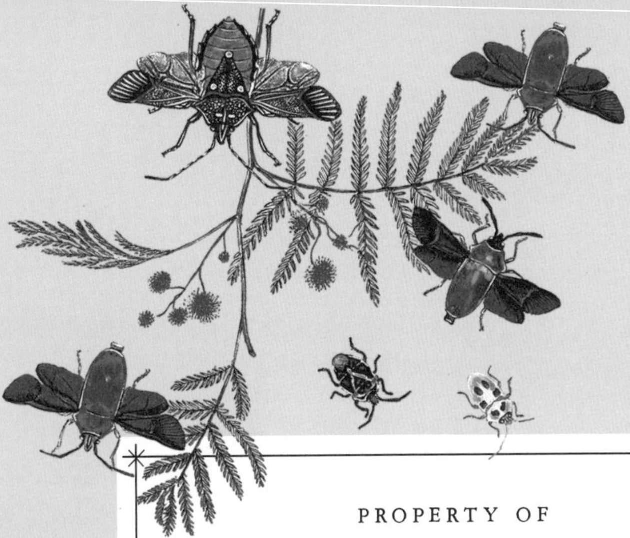

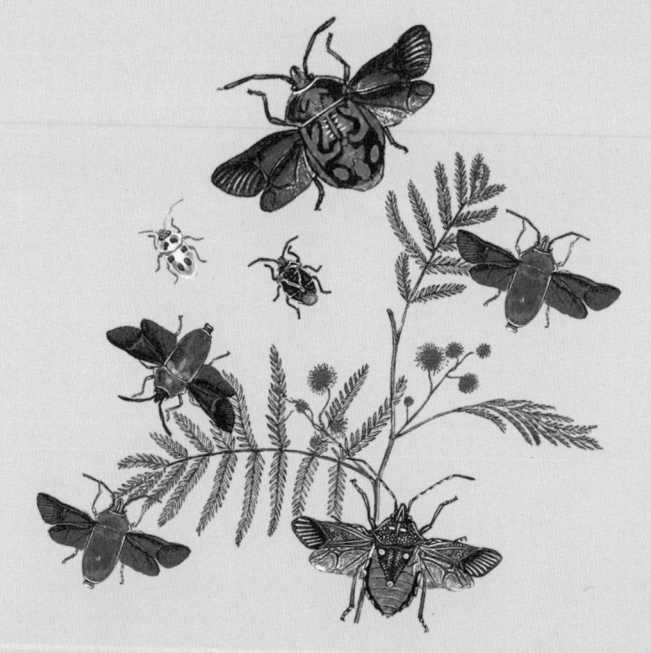

PROPERTY OF
_____

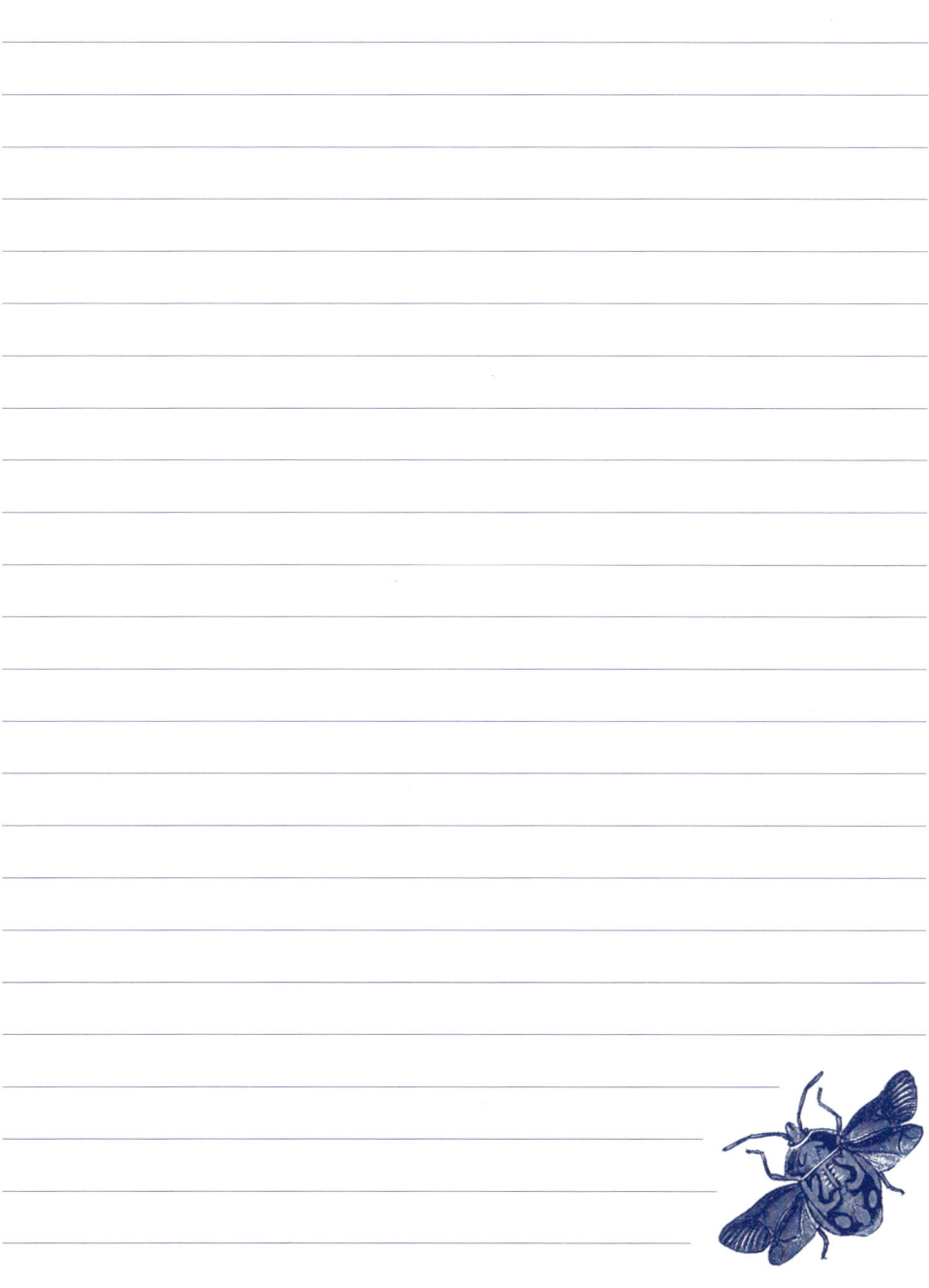

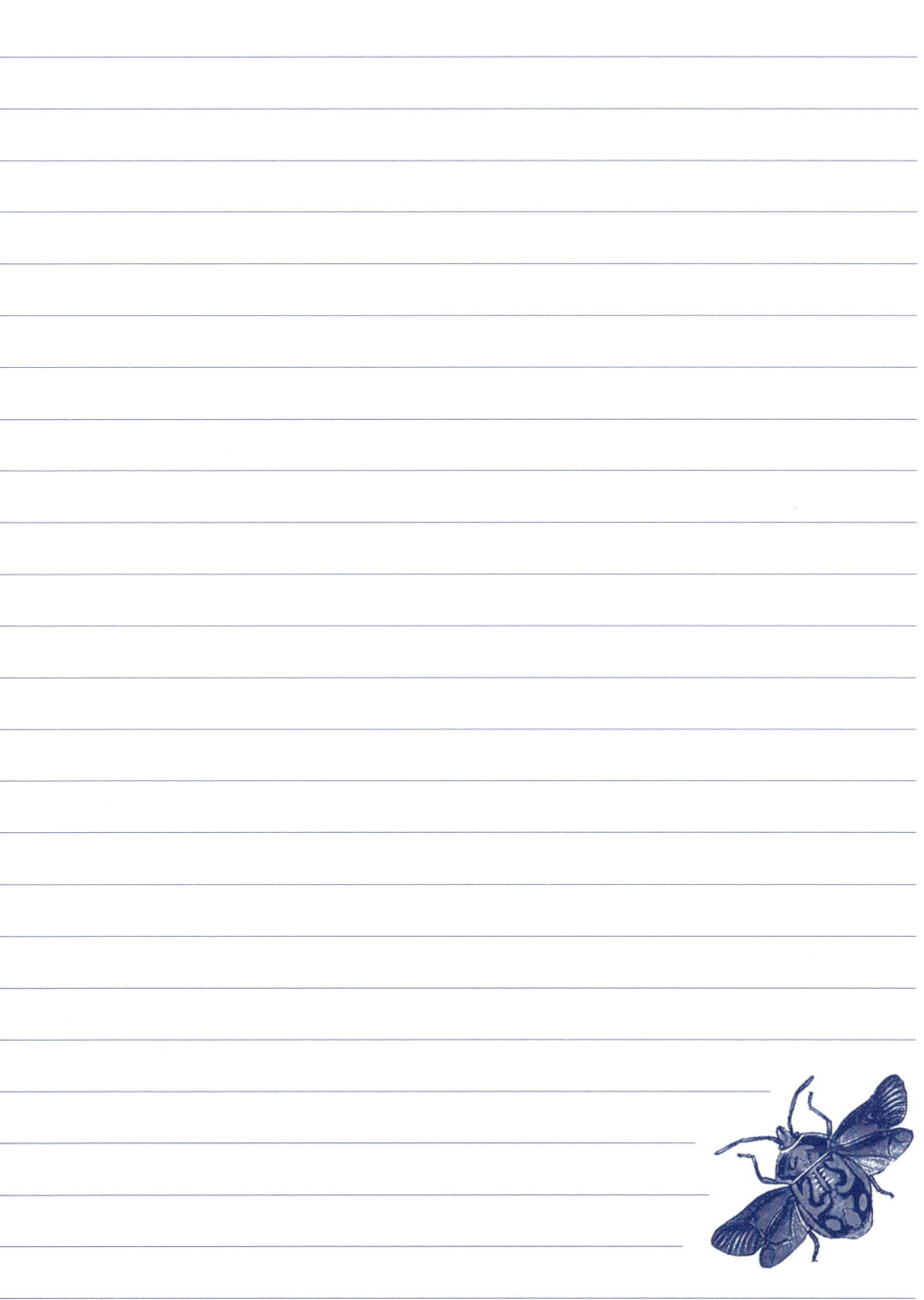

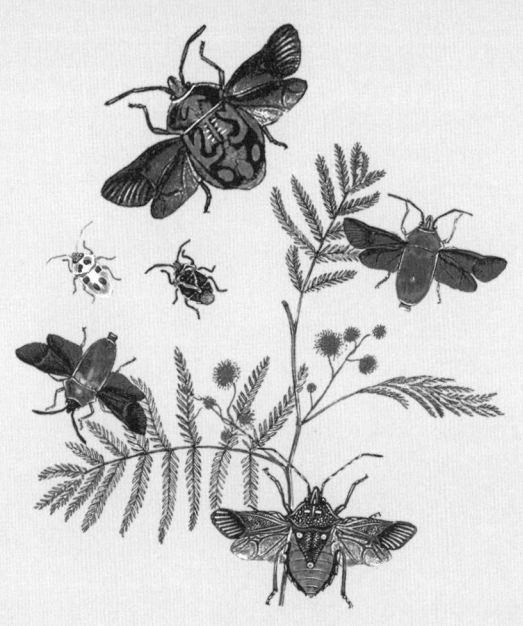

ART OF NATURE
Botanical Collection

INSIGHTS
an imprint of
INSIGHT EDITIONS
www.insighteditions.com

Copyright © 2021 Insight Editions.
All rights reserved.

MANUFACTURED IN CHINA

10 9 8 7 6 5 4 3 2